FOOTPRINTS

William K. Durr
Jean M. LePere
Mary Lou Alsin

CONSULTANT: Paul McKee

HOUGHTON MIFFLIN COMPANY · Bost

Atlanta · Dallas · Geneva, Illinois · Hopewell, New Jer

Illustrated by: CHRIS CZERNOTA
KEVIN CALLAHAN · JARED LEE
HILARY HAYTON · BILL MORRISON

1978 IMPRESSION

Copyright © 1976 by Houghton Mifflin Company

Printed in the U.S.A.
ISBN: 0-395-20405-4

Contents

Marty, the TV Dog

Peppy: Marty! Marty!

Look at the man in the TV truck.

He is going to your house.

Marty: My TV is working, Peppy.

That man can't be going to my house.

What will he do there?

Peppy: We will have to find out.

Marty: Look what he is doing to the TV!

It isn't working now!

What will I do without TV, Peppy?

Peppy: You can come out and run with me.

Marty: I don't like to run.

I like to look at TV.

6

Peppy: You can't look at TV.

What will you do now, Marty?

Marty: I don't know what I'll do, Peppy.

What can a dog like me do?

Peppy: I know.

We can go for a walk.

And you'll forget the TV.

Marty: What is in there, Peppy?

Peppy: I don't know.

But we can find out.

It looks like fun to me.

Marty: But we can't go in there.

That man will see us.

Peppy: We can get in this way, Marty.

That man will not see us here.

Marty: Peppy! Look! A TV!

What a big TV!

Peppy: It is big.

And look at the dog in the picture.

Marty: The TV man can have my little TV.

I can come here and look at this one.

Peppy: Marty! Look!

That man will get us.

We have to get out of here.

Marty: But I can't go now, Peppy.

How will I see the picture?

Man: Dogs can't be in here.

Now get out!

And don't come back!

Marty: I'm going back in there.

I want to look at that big TV.

Peppy: Marty, you can't go back in there.

You know that.

Marty: I'm going back in there.

Peppy: Marty, you can't go back.

That man will get you.

Marty: The TV at my house isn't working.

You know how much I like TV.

He will not see us go in this way.

Peppy: You and your big TV!
Now look where we are!

Marty: Do you know where we're going?
Will we have TV there?
You know how much I like TV.

Peppy: There's no TV where we are going!

Man: OK, you dogs!
Get out of there.

Peppy: Do you know where we are, Marty?
I'm scared to look.

Marty: We're back at my house!
It's nice to be back here.

Peppy: Marty, your TV is working.

What a nice surprise.

Now you can look at TV.

Marty: You know what, Peppy?

I'm going to forget TV.

And go for a run with you.

Peppy: That is a nice surprise!

Bill: I like to walk dogs.

Walking little dogs is fun.

And it's not much work.

Lucy: But we don't get much for doing it.

I want to walk big dogs.

Bill: Look at that dog!

He's a big one.

Lucy: Can we walk your nice big dog?

Mrs. Lee: You can walk Chester.

But I'll tell you this now.

He isn't much of a walker.

He likes to run.

Lucy: How can Chester run?

He can't see much, can he?

Mrs. Lee: He can see where he's going.

It's no problem for Chester to run.

Chester's biggest problem is walking.

Bill: He will walk for us.

Lucy: He's going to get away!

Bill: Look at that dog go!
We'll have to stop him.

Lucy: Stop, Chester! Stop!

Bill: Now we have a problem.

Do you see where that dog is?

And here comes a bus!

Oh! I'm scared to look at him!

Lucy: You can look now.

The bus stopped.

Police Officer: Come and get your dog.

Lucy: He's not my dog.

This is Chester.

Get up, Chester! Get up!

You have to get up!

Man: Take this hot dog.

A hot dog will get him up.

Lucy: Come here, Chester.

Come and get the hot dog.

Bill: He's going to get up.

He wants it.

Bill: Oh, no! He's going into the library!

He can't take a hot dog in there!

Lucy: What a dog!

Bill: Chester! Chester!

Mrs. Way: Chester isn't in here.

No boy is in the library.

Now take your dogs out of here.

Lucy: Chester is not a boy.

He's a dog.

And we have to take him for a walk.

Lucy: I see Chester!

Mrs. Way: You'll have to take him out!

Bill: He will not get up for us.
.How can we take him out?

Lucy: I'll go and get help.

Lucy: Chester is in the library.

Mrs. Lee: You walk dogs in the library?

Lucy: No. Chester is in there.
And now we can't get him out.

Mrs. Lee: We'll get Chester out of the library.

Lucy: Walking big dogs isn't much fun.

Bill: No more big dogs for us!

Lucy: Big dogs are a big problem!

Find the **runner.**

Where is the **ticket taker?**

Find the **waiter.**

Where is the **player?**

Find the **dog walker.**

Ann: I want to go in that rabbit.

I want to go and see the real lions.

Dad: You can't go without me.

And I have to wait here for Mom.

Mike: Ted and I will go.

And Ann can go with us.

We can look after Ann.

Ann: You don't have to look after me.

Dad: Here are the tickets for the Jungle Bus.
Have fun.
I'll wait here for you.

Ted: It's fun to be up here.

Ted: The bus is stopping.

We're in the jungle now.

Look at how much there is to see.

Ann: Where is the kangaroo?

Mike: Here she is!

Isn't the little kangaroo nice?

Ann: I like this jungle more and more.

Ted: Look at the tiger, Mike.

Ann: I want to play with the little lion.

Mike: You can't play with the lion, Ann.

Ted: The big lion will not like that.

Mike: Now Ann wants to play with a tiger.

Ann! You have to come with us.

We want to see more animals.

Ted: We have to go back now.

There's a bus we can take.

Man: Do you have tickets?

Ted: No, we don't have tickets.

Man: You can get tickets there.

Ted: Now we have a problem.

How will we get back without tickets?

Ann: Dad will come and get us.

Mike: No, Ann.

Mom and Dad are waiting for us.

Ann: I'll tell you what we can do.

Mike: You are little, Ann.
How can you know what to do?

Ann: I know what we can do.
Look! Do you see the bus up there?
We can walk back the way it is going.

Mike: We can't wait here.

Ted: And the bus is going back that way.

Ann: I know it will work.
Come with me and you'll find out.

Ann: Here we are.

Dad: We have waited and waited for you.
How did you get here?

Mom: You didn't come back on a bus.

Ted: The bus tickets are one-way tickets.

Mike: We walked back.

Mom: How did you know the way back?

Mike: We walked the way the bus comes.

Dad: You are lucky, Ann.
The boys did look after you.

Ann: Oh, no, Dad!
The boys did not look after me!
I looked after the boys.
Ted and Mike are the lucky ones.

Rabbit: Here comes Turtle.

This is my lucky day.

Now I'll have fun.

Rabbit: Come and run with me, Turtle.

We can run to the schoolhouse.

I'm going to win!

Turtle: But I want to win.

Rabbit: You're not going to win.

It's my lucky day.

It's not your lucky day!

Cat: Rabbit, will you stop and help me?
My truck is in there.

Rabbit: I'm not stopping now, Cat.
Turtle and I are running to the school.
It's my lucky day.
And I'm going to win.

Cat: What will I do without my truck?

Rabbit: That's your problem!

Cat: Can you get my truck, Turtle?

Turtle: I can't stop, Cat.
I'm running with Rabbit.

Cat: But my truck is in there.
And I can't get it out.
I really have to have my truck.

Turtle: You do have a problem.
I'll go in and get your truck.

46

Turtle: Here it is, Cat.

And now I'll be on my way.

Cat: You are really a big help, Turtle.

I want you to win.

Dog: Help! Help!

Can you do something to help me?

Rabbit: I'm running to the school with Turtle.

I can't help you now, Dog.

Dog: Will you help me?

Rabbit didn't stop for me.

Turtle: Can you wait, Dog?

I'm running with Rabbit now.

And Rabbit is way up there.

I'll come back and help you.

Dog: Don't go, Turtle.

I'm really hot here.

And I can't wait for you to come back.

Turtle: OK, Dog.

I'll help you.

Dog: It was nice of you to help me.

Run after Rabbit now.

I really want you to win!

Rabbit: Turtle, come here.

I'm in here.

And I can't get out.

Turtle: Oh, there you are, Rabbit.

What are you doing in there?

Rabbit: I was looking back at you and Dog.

And I didn't see where I was going.

Help me get out of here.

Turtle: I don't know, Rabbit.

I had to stop and help Cat.

And then I had to help Dog.

Now you want me to stop and help you.

This is not my lucky day.

Rabbit: Turtle, help me!

Help me get out of here.

Turtle: OK, Rabbit.

I'll help you.

I know how to get you out.

Turtle: See, Rabbit.

This is getting you out of there.

Rabbit: I'm going to win after all!

Cat: You win, Turtle!

Dog: You win! You win!

Turtle: How did I win?
All I did was stop.

Rabbit: I was going to win, Turtle.
But you had all the luck.

see help

library look

zoo house

run go

smile school

RED IS NICE

Mike: Do you want to go to the library, Bill?

Bill: I can't go with you now.

Do you see my tree house?

I have to paint it red.

Mike: I know how to paint tree houses.

I can help you paint it.

Then we can go to the library.

Mike: This really looks good!

Red is a good color for a tree house.

Bill: Oh, no!

Now there's paint on the doghouse!

Bill: I know what we can do.

My dad got all this red paint for me.

Red is a good color for a doghouse.

We'll paint the doghouse red.

Mike: I'm really getting sick of painting.

Bill: We can't stop now.

Bill: There! The doghouse is painted.

Mike: We got red paint on the fence!
Do we have more paint?

Bill: Yes. We'll have to paint the fence.

Mike: Red is a good color for a fence.
We'll paint the fence.
Then we can go to the library.

Bill: This will surprise my dad!

Mike: I'm hot, and I'm sick of painting. Can we go to the library now?

Bill: No. We have to get this painted. Get to work.

Bill: There! The fence is red.

Mike: Will your dad like it?

Bill: We'll find out.

Here he comes now.

Dad: What's going on here, boys?

Bill: I had to paint my tree house.

And paint got on the doghouse.

Mike: Then we had to paint the doghouse.

Bill: And paint got on the fence.
Then we had to paint the fence.

Mike: Oh, Bill! We got paint on the house.

Bill: We'll have to paint the house.
Red is a good color for a house.

Dad: Look, boys!

There's red paint on you!

We'll have to paint you.

Bill: Oh, no! Red isn't a good color for me.

Mike: I don't want to be painted red.

Dad: And I don't want a red house!

DINOSAURS IN THE PARK

Lucy: Do you want to play school, Bill?

Bill: I can't play school now, Lucy.

I'm going to the park.

I'm going to see some dinosaurs.

Lucy: Don't be funny, Bill.

There are no more real dinosaurs.

I have a dinosaur book.

And I know.

Bill: Oh, yes, there are!

Read this.

Lucy: Where did you get this, Bill?

Bill: I got it in the park.

It was on one of the trees.

Lucy: What are dinosaurs doing in the park?

Bill: I don't know.

But we'll have to find out.

Lucy: What's going on?

What are all the girls and boys doing?

Bill: There's a TV man, Lucy.

Hot Dog Man: It's the Dinosaurs.

They all want to see the Dinosaurs.

Lucy: They can't be real dinosaurs.

Bill: We're looking for the dinosaurs.

Did you see some here?

Girl: Yes, I did.

Lucy: You did! Where?

Girl: In back of that red fence.

That's where you'll find the Dinosaurs.

Bill: Don't you want to go in, Lucy?

Don't you want to see real dinosaurs?

Lucy: There are no more real dinosaurs.

I read that in my dinosaur book.

Bill: I'm going in.

Bill: What's that funny noise?

Man: It's the Dinosaurs playing.
Oh, what a noise!

Lucy: But it can't be dinosaurs!

Bill: Where are the dinosaurs?

Boy: The Dinosaurs are playing up there.

Bill: This is really funny!

Lucy: They are Dinosaurs!
But they aren't in my book.

What can you make that you can't see?

Noise

What is the name of a wet pet?

Fish

The more you take away
The bigger it gets.
What is it?

A hole

73

REAL DINOSAURS

There are no real dinosaurs now.

Here are some pictures of real dinosaurs.

You can see how big they are.

Look at this dinosaur name.

BRONTOSAURUS

Dinosaur names are big, too.

Can you find the dinosaurs in the picture?

Dinosaurs liked the jungle.

It was hot and green there.

Look at the house in the picture.

Look at the man in the picture.

See how much bigger the dinosaur is!

This dinosaur was one of the biggest.

Now look at this picture.

See the man with the dog?

The dinosaur here is little.

It was one of the littlest dinosaurs.

What is this girl doing?

The girl in this picture is working.

She can tell you what dinosaurs did.

She knows how big a dinosaur was.

And what dinosaur teeth looked like.

But she wants to know more.

And she is here to find out.

How do we know what dinosaurs are like?
We can go in here to find out.

Have you seen a dinosaur like this one?

There are parks with dinosaur footprints.
You can walk where a dinosaur walked.
The footprints are real!

DINOSAUR
NATIONAL
MONUMENT

Get a dinosaur book at the library.

Read it.

And look at the pictures.

Then you can do something like this.